Contents

TO THE FADELESS MEMORY OF OUR HEROIC DEAD AND TO THOSE WHO HAVE LOST THIS BRIEF VOLUME OF SKETCH AND STORY IS DEDICATED, IN UNSTINTED ADMIRATION, IN AFFECTIONATE SYMPATHY, AND IN THE UNSHAKEABLE BELIEF THAT 5

PREFACE 9

INTRODUCTION 13

'Over the Top' 17
FROM 'THERE' TO 'HERE' 17
AUSTRALIANS—IN VARIOUS MOODS 23
    IMPROMPTU WIT. 24
    MORE CURIOUS THAN CAUTIOUS. 25
    IT'S ALL IN THE GAME. 25
    A CLEVER RUSE. 26
    TURNING THE TABLES. 26
    HEROISM UNEXCELLED. 27
    'WE WERE PALS.' 27

SUNDAY, 'SOMEWHERE IN FRANCE' 29

SOLDIERS' SUPERSTITIONS 33

ON THE EVE OF BATTLE 39
    TO THE WIDOWS OF FRANCE 39
        FOOTNOTES: 40

'OVER THE TOP.'	41
SHELLS: A FEW SMILES AND A CONTRAST	47
MESSINES	53
JUNE 7, 1917	53
BILL THE BUGLER	57
A TRAGEDY OF THE WAR	59
RECREATION BEHIND THE LINES	63
FOR THE CAUSE OF THE EMPIRE	69
OUR HEROIC DEAD	71
THE SILVER LINING	73

Major-General Sir John Monash, K.C.B., V.D.
Photo by Elliott & Fry.

TO THE FADELESS MEMORY OF OUR HEROIC DEAD AND TO THOSE WHO HAVE LOST THIS BRIEF VOLUME OF SKETCH AND STORY IS DEDICATED, IN UNSTINTED ADMIRATION, IN AFFECTIONATE SYMPATHY, AND IN THE UNSHAKEABLE BELIEF THAT

'As sure as God's in heaven,
As sure as He stands for right,
As sure as the Hun this wrong hath done,
So surely we'll win this fight.'

PREFACE

PREFACE

In response to numerous requests from the 'boys,' this brief volume of story and sketch is published. It makes no pretension to literary merit, neither is it intended to serve as a history of the Division. The indulgence of those who may read is earnestly solicited, in view of the work having been prepared amidst the trying and thrilling experiences so common to active service. The fighting history of the Australian Forces is one long series of magnificent achievements, beginning on that day of sacred and glorious memory, April 25, 1915. Ever since that wonderful test of capacity and courage the Australians have advanced from victory to victory, and have won for themselves a splendid reputation. Details of training, raids, engagements, and tactical features have been purposely omitted. The more serious aspect will be written by others. In deference to Mr. Censor, names of places and persons have been suppressed, but such omissions will not detract from the interest of the book. 'Over the Top with the Third Australian Division' is illustrative of that big-hearted, devil-may-care style of the Australians, the men who can see the brighter side of life under the most distracting circumstances and most unpromising conditions. In the pages that follow, some incidents of the life of the men may help to pass away a pleasant hour and serve as a reminder of events, past and gone, but which will ever be fresh to those whose immediate interests attach to the Third Australian Division.

G.P. CUTTRISS.

The Author.
Photo by Lafayette, Ltd.

INTRODUCTION

INTRODUCTION

At the outbreak of the World War in August, 1914, the Australian as a soldier was an unknown quantity. It is quite true that in the previous campaigns in the Soudan and in South Africa, Australia had been represented, and that a sprinkling of native-born Australians had taken service in the Imperial armies. The performances of these pioneers of Australia in arms were creditable, and the reputation which they had earned was full of promise. But, viewed in their proper perspective, these contributions to Imperial Defence were no true index of the capacity of the Australian nation to raise and maintain a great army worthy and able in all details to take its place in a world war, beside the armies of the great and historic civilizations of the Old World.

No Australian, nor least of all those among them who had laboured in times of peace to prepare the way for a great national effort, whenever the call to action should come, ever doubted the capacity of the nation worthily to respond; but while the magnitude and quality of the possible effort might well have been doubted by our Imperial authorities and our Allies, and while it was certainly regarded as negligible by our enemies, the result in achievement has exceeded, in a mighty degree, the most optimistic hopes even of those who knew or thought they knew what Australia was capable of.

For, to-day, Australia has, besides its substantial contribution to the Naval Forces of the Empire, actually in being a land army of five divisions and two mounted divisions, fully officered, fully equipped, and stamped with the seal of brilliantly successful performance; and has created and maintained all the hundred and one national activities upon which such an achievement depends.

We are still too close to the picture to realize the miracle which has been wrought, or to understand in all their breadth the factors on which it has depended; but, fundamentally, and overshadowing all other factors, the result is based upon the character of the Australian people, and upon the personality of the Australian soldier.

It is the latter factor which, to one who has been for so long in intimate daily contact with him, makes the closest appeal. It is from that close association, from the knowledge born of experience of him in every phase of his daily life, that the Australian can be proclaimed as second to none in the world both as a soldier and as a fighting man. For these things are not synonymous, and the first lesson that every recruit has to learn is that they are not synonymous; that the thing which converts a mere fighting man into a soldier is the sense of discipline. This word 'discipline' is often cruelly misused and misunderstood. Upon it, in its broadest and truest sense, depends the capacity of men, in the aggregate, for successful concerted action. It is precisely because the Australian is born with and develops in his national life the very instinct of discipline that he has been enabled to prove himself so successful a soldier. He obeys constituted authority because he knows that success depends upon his doing so, whether his activities are devoted to the interests of his football team or his industrial organization or his regiment. He has an infinite capacity for 'team' work. And he brings to bear upon that work a high order of intelligence and understanding. In his other splendid qualities, his self-reliance, his devotion to his cause and his comrades, and his unfailing cheerfulness under hardship and distress, he displays other manifestations of that same instinct of discipline.

Some day cold and formal histories will record the deeds and performances of the Australian soldiery; but it is not to them that we shall turn for an illumination of his true character. It is to stories such as these which follow, of his daily life, of his psychology, of his personality, that we must look. And we shall look not in vain, when, as in the following pages, the tale has been written down by one of themselves, who has lived and worked among them, and who understands them in a spirit of true sympathy and comradeship. The Author of these sketches is himself true to his type, and an embodiment of all that is most worthy and most admirable in the Australian soldier.

JOHN MONASH, *Major-General.*

'Over the Top'

FROM 'THERE' TO 'HERE'

Towards the end of November, 1916, our hopes of moving out from 'where we then were' to 'where we now are' materialized to the evident satisfaction of all. Few, if any, cared as to our probable destination; the chief interest centred in the fact that we were to start for the Front. The time spent Somewhere in the Motherland was by no means wasted. Due regard had been paid to the training of the men, who reached a standard of efficiency which earned for the Division a reputation second to none. While in England the Third was the subject of scorn and bitter criticism. Older Divisions could not forget, and possibly regretted, the fact that they had had no such prolonged training in mock trenches and in inglorious safety. However, since leaving England the Division has lived down the scorn that was heaped upon it, by upholding the traditions handed down by older and more war-worn units. Recently the Division was referred to by a noted General as one of the best equipped and most efficient units not only amongst the Overseas Divisions but of the whole Army in France.

The arrangements for our moving out were approximately perfect. There was no hitch. The military machine, like the Tanks of recent fame, over-rides or brushes to one side all obstacles. There was manifest among all ranks an eagerness to leave nothing undone that would in any way facilitate entraining and embarkation. The knowledge that we were at last on our way to the 'Dinkum' thing had the effect of leading us to take a more serious view of the situation. It is surprising, however, how soon men become attached to a place; and though the conditions at Lark Hill were in no sense ideal, it had been our home for several months and we were loth to leave. Perhaps the thought that many of us might possibly never return inspired the longing looks that were directed towards the camp as we marched on our way to the station. Who of those who took part in that march will forget the cheers with which we were greeted by the residents of that picturesquely situated village as we trudged along its winding road? We had enjoyed their hospitality, and we appreciated their cordial wishes for success and safety.

The task of entraining a large body of men was expertly accomplished, and after a brief delay we were speeding in the direction of the port of embarkation. The train journey was practically without event. The men were disposed to be quiet. On arrival at the quay parties were detailed to assist in putting mails and equipment aboard the transports. Punctually at the hour advised we trooped aboard the ships that were to convey us across the water. There was very little accommodation for men, but they squeezed in and made the best of the situation. The trip across was not as comfortable as it might have been, but its duration was so brief that the discomfort was scarcely worth serious thought. The transports cast anchor off the harbour early the following morning, but it was not until late in the afternoon that they were berthed alongside the wharf. Scarcely had the transports touched the wharfside when they commenced to disgorge their living freight.

The trip across was not as comfortable as it might have been.

From the waterside we marched to No. 1 Rest (?) Camp, situated on the summit of a hill on the outskirts of the town. The camp was reached some time after darkness had settled down over the land. The weather was most miserable. The air was charged with icy blasts, and rain fell continuously throughout the night. The least said about our impressions and experiences during our brief stay in that camp the better; suffice to state that one of the most miserable memories that can be recalled in connexion with our experiences on active service is associated with No. 1 Rest Camp.

The following morning we marched to the main railway station and entrained for the Front. The accommodation provided was fairly comfortable, though the carriages (?) had been used more for carrying mules than men. The train journey extended over thirty hours. All along the route there were evidences of military activity denoting extensive and effective military organization. We noted the continuous stream of traffic on the roads, and were amused with the names chalked on the heavy guns, which were being drawn by a style of tractor quite new to most of us. 'No friend of Fritz' was a powerful-looking gun, and greatly impressed us; but the sight of a number of heavier guns thrilled us, and we involuntarily shouted 'Good old England.'

There was not a dull moment during that thirty hours' run. There was much to interest the 'freshmen.' Eventually we reached our rail destination, and marched to our quarters, where we arrived late at night. That we were not far from the fighting line was very evident by the close proximity of the artillery, which expressed itself so emphatically that the air reverberated with its deep boom, relieved at intervals by the staccato reports of machine-guns in action.

The troops were quartered in different places. They were as indifferent as they were different, but any place which afforded shelter from the rain and protection from the cold was greatly appreciated. Despite the inconveniences within and the noises without few had difficulty in wooing Morpheus and reposed in his embrace until a late hour next morning.

Opportunity was afforded during the day for having a look round and cultivating an acquaintance with the district. The country round about is fairly level, and, despite the fact that it was just behind the lines and under enemy observation, farming operations and business were carried on in perfect serenity. A cinema afforded entertainment in the evenings. The men were cheerful, and accepted the change from the 'sham' to the real uncomplainingly, and commenced making their billets as comfortable as circumstances would permit. Stoves were greatly in demand, but few were available. The law in France is that nothing shall be removed from a building without permission. Troops were forbidden to enter houses under any pretence whatever; but very occasionally men lost their way, and unwittingly (?) wandered into forbidden places, and when detected by certain officials evinced great surprise on being found therein. The Town Major on one occasion was walking past a building, the door of which was ajar, and he observed two men struggling with a stove half up the stairway. 'What are you doing with that stove?' he peremptorily asked. 'Putting it back, sir,' was the prompt reply.

Church buildings seem to have received special attention from enemy artillery.

It is surprising with what readiness the Australian adapts himself to whatever conditions prevail. He possesses plenty of initiative, which is an invaluable asset on active service. Friendships were quickly formed with the villagers, who were chiefly refugees, and much amusement was caused as the troops sought to make use of the French words which they had endeavoured to learn. There was scarcely any necessity, however to try to speak French, as most of the people understood sufficient of the English language for ordinary business transactions. It was only when love-making was resorted to that a knowledge of French became a vital necessity.

There was a great deal to interest the troops in this district, which for a brief period had been occupied by the enemy. The town was subjected to heavy shell fire almost daily. Evidences of the enemy's brief stay and the effects of their 'frightfulness' were not lacking. Since our occupation, the place has been reduced to a heap of ruins by the enemy's artillery, which appears to have paid special attention to church buildings, for many of them have been totally destroyed. Almost immediately upon our arrival in this place certain units of the Division occupied the trenches along the Divisional Front, and very soon proved themselves to be just as capable as the more experienced troops which they had relieved.

We were located in and about the town for several months, during which time the Third Division won a name for the efficiency and daring of its raids, and silenced for all time the gibes and criticisms of the more war-worn comrades of the older divisions. 'Here' the Division has comported itself precisely as it did over 'there.' In training the men tried to do their duty. In battle they have done their duty, many of them even unto death.

FROM 'THERE' TO 'HERE'

When you are perfectly sober, and you imagine you're not.

What of the future? Just the same; but with that courage and confidence born of experience, still greater attainments may be expected.

AUSTRALIANS—IN VARIOUS MOODS

The Australian soldier is a peculiar mixture; but for pluck in the face of danger, patience in the grip of pain, and initiative in the presence of the unexpected, he holds a unique place amongst men. He has been subjected to considerable adverse criticism for seeming lack of discipline. Kind things and other kinds of things have been freely said to his detriment; but if every word were true, he is not to blame. The Australian soldier, like any other soldier, is but the product of a system, the standard or inefficiency of which it would not be just to hold him responsible for. The majority frankly admit that soldiering is not in their line. They would never choose it as a profession; yet the man from 'Down Under' has given unmistakable proof that he is as amenable to discipline as any other, and rightly led he, as a fighting force, compares favourably with the best that any nation has produced. His language at times is not too choice. It is said that on occasions the outburst has been so hot that the water carts have been consumed in flames. Be that as it may, his diction in no sense denotes the exact state of his mind or morals. His contagious cheerfulness has established him a firm favourite with the French people, whose admiration and affection he will hold for all time.

An officer belonging to another part of the Empire tells a story against himself. Arriving in a village late at night, he inquired at a cottage as to whether a billet could be provided. Before replying the occupant, a widow, asked whether he was an Australian or a ——. Upon learning his regimental identity, she told him that she had no accommodation. Somewhat vexed, he retorted, 'If I were an Australian you would probably have found room for me.' 'Yes,' was her reply. 'Well,' the officer observed, 'I fail to understand what you see in the Australians; they're savages.' Before closing the door the occupant said, 'I like savages.'

The following incidents but imperfectly portray the irrepressible humour, unexampled heroism, and splendid initiative so commendably displayed by the Australian under the varying and trying conditions common to modern warfare.

IMPROMPTU WIT.

The ——th Battalion had been relieved. The men had been in the lines six days. They looked forward to a few days' spell at the back of the trenches. On reaching the back area some of the men were detailed to carry supplies up to the lines. Whilst so engaged they were met by a General, who was in the habit of visiting the trenches unaccompanied. This officer, himself a young man, ever had a cheery word for the 'boys.' One of the men on duty lagged some distance behind the main party. The expression on his face indicated that he was 'fed up.' He was also beginning to feel the weight of the sack which he was carrying. As he passed, the General acknowledged the reluctant turn of his head by way of salute, and then asked, 'Where are you going, my man?' 'In the —— knees, sir,' was the ready and witty reply.

'Where are you going, my man?'
'In the knees, sir.'

MORE CURIOUS THAN CAUTIOUS.

A man on duty in the front-line trenches displayed more curiosity than caution and eventually paid the penalty for his mistake. In the endeavour to ascertain what was going on across 'no man's way,' he exposed himself to the keen observation of an enemy sniper, who quickly trained his rifle on him and a bullet penetrated the steel helmet of the over-curious soldier. The bullet traversed the crown of the head and lodged in the nape of the neck. He flung his rifle to one side and did a sprint along the duck-boards. His mates inquired the reason of his haste. Without abating his speed he called out, 'Do you think that I want to drop dead in that blimey mud?' As he reached the dry duck-boards his strength gave out, and he would have fallen but for the timely assistance from two of his mates, who lowered him gently, then brought a stretcher on which to carry him to the R.A.P. As they were about to start away with him, he opened his eyes, and they inquired if he were hurt. 'Well, it does give you a bit of a headache, you know,' he replied; 'have you got a fag?' A cigarette was handed to him, and as they carried him away he smoked his 'fag.'

IT'S ALL IN THE GAME.

A similar instance of absolute self-forgetfulness and indomitable spirit occurred at another part of the line. A shell burst near to our wire and projected a tangled heap of it forward. A piece of barbed wire encircled a man's neck. The barbs bit into the flesh. The shoulders of his tunic were torn. The blood flowed freely from nasty cuts in his neck and cheeks. Without altering his position he looked out in the direction of the Hun lines and declared that if he ever got hold of the —— Hun who fired that —— shell, he would drive his —— bayonet through him. When the wire was taken from round his neck, his face wreathed in smiles as he remarked, 'Well, I suppose it is all in the game,' then turning to his mates he asked, 'I say, digger, have you got a smoke?'

My Lady Nicotine is certainly a general favourite amongst the 'boys.' They seek her solace during the critical periods of their active service life. Unquestionably one of the most deeply appreciated issues that the men receive is that of tobacco and cigarettes. For this extra 'ration' credit must be given to the A.C.F. and other funds which have expended large sums of money in making available to the troops the 'pipe of peace' and the comfort of the 'fag.'

A CLEVER RUSE.

This incident is related in the strictest confidence, and solely upon the condition that the identity of the individuals concerned will not be disclosed. A certain officer—I dare not mention his rank, as there are so few Generals amongst us that to even mention it would be tantamount to disclosing his identity. Therefore, a certain officer was on a tour of inspection. The utmost effort had been made by the unit holding the line to have everything satisfactory. The trenches must be kept clean and sanitary. Every precaution is adopted to safeguard the health of the men. The officer's visit was timed just after the issue of rum had been made. Rum is not a regular issue by any means, but a little had been made available at that time, and was supposed to be taken much the same as is medicine, viz., on the M.O.'s recommendation. A few minutes before the arrival of the officer of high rank the platoon officer observed one of his men under the influence of drink. He learned on inquiry that the man had secured some rum in addition to what had been issued. To get him out of the way was his first thought. Somebody suggested that he be placed on a stretcher and covered with a blanket. It was no sooner suggested than acted upon. When the officer making the inspection entered the trench two men bore the stretcher with its burden past him. He stood to one side and saluted as he would the dead. Of course the man on the stretcher was dead—'dead drunk.' No questions were asked, therefore no untruths were told. The unit had the satisfaction of learning that their lines were satisfactory; but in a certain company's orderly-room the following morning a certain man had a most unenviable quarter of an hour in the presence of his irate O.C.

TURNING THE TABLES.

During a raid made on our lines the enemy succeeded in reaching our trenches, but were quickly ejected. Two of the raiding party were killed, and as many were taken prisoners. One of them met his death in a very tragic manner. A member of the ——th battalion was fast asleep in his makeshift of a dugout the night the Germans entered our lines. He knew nothing of their visit until wakened by a heavy hand being placed on his shoulder. Great was his astonishment on waking to find himself gazing into the face of a Hun, who gurgled and gesticulated, which sounds and signs he interpreted as an invitation to put his hands up. His hands went up as he struggled to his feet. He then discovered that he was about six inches taller than his captor and certainly much heavier. When they got out on the duck-boards, the prisoner suddenly looked down and allowed his gaze to rest on the boards at his feet. The German's curiosity was aroused, and he fell into the trap set for him. He made the fatal mistake of allowing his gaze to be diverted from the prisoner to the duck-boards. By a quick movement the prisoner possessed himself of his captor's rifle. One blow from a tightly-clenched fist sufficed to lay him his length along the boards, and the next moment the would-be captor was breathing his last with his own bayonet through his chest, and the Australian was heard to remark, 'I'll teach the blighter to waken me from my sleep.'

HEROISM UNEXCELLED.

It would be invidious to single out one for special mention from the great army of brave men who have upheld the traditions of the Empire on the field of battle. Without mentioning the name of the hero the following incident is cited as illustrative of many which speak eloquently of the bravery of our 'boys.' Our lines were being furiously shelled, and a member of a certain battalion was severely wounded. Assisted by another stretcher-bearer, the hero of this incident endeavoured to convey the wounded man to the A.D.S. The trench along which they were walking was blown in, making it necessary to carry the injured man 'over the top.' This was done in full view of the enemy. While so engaged a 'Minnie' was observed coming over, and warning was given for all to get under cover. All did except Private ——, who, actuated by an impulse to protect a fallen comrade, and without thought for his own safety, immediately threw himself upon the wounded man to protect him. For this gallant act he was awarded the Military Medal.

A couple of months later this same person was in the trenches when a British 'plane was compelled to land in a very exposed and shell-swept area. Both occupants of the machine rushed for the trenches. The observer reached a place of safety, but the pilot, who was wounded, fell exhausted. Without thought of personal safety, and despite the fact that the Germans were shelling the machine, the stretcher-bearer climbed 'over the top,' in full view of the enemy, and carried the wounded pilot to a shell-hole, where he rendered first-aid and then brought the injured man to the safety of our trenches. For this further act of bravery he was awarded a bar to his M.M.

'WE WERE PALS.'

A man came to the D.B.O. just after a certain engagement in connexion with which the Australians did splendid work. They secured a great victory. They got to their objectives on time and took quite a large number of prisoners. Every victory has its price, and it was concerning part of the price of victory that the young man had made the visit. He told of his pal, a D.C.M. man, who had been killed, whose body was lying out on the ridge. He wished to know whether arrangements could be made for the body to be brought down to a back area cemetery for burial. Whenever practicable such is done. The D.B.O. made inquiries, and learned that no transport was available. The roads were in a frightful condition, and in view of the incessant enemy shelling of the area, decided that the body would have to be buried in the vicinity of where it had fallen. Arrangements were made for the man to return on the morrow for the purpose of acting as guide to the Padre who would conduct the service. Next day, he came to the Burials Officer. Surprise was evinced at the change in his appearance. His uniform was covered with mud and wet through, and he seemed to be quite exhausted. 'I have come about the burial, sir,' he said. 'Could it be fixed up for this afternoon, I have brought the body down?' Upon making inquiries as to how he had managed it, he replied that he and another had asked permission to go out and bring the body in. It meant a carry over broken ground of about five miles, under heavy shell fire most of the distance; but these faithful comrades gladly endured the hardship and braved the dangers to ensure the burial of their deceased mate in a cemetery which is one of the few that has not been disturbed by the bursting shell. Thinking that the deceased was a near relative of this brave lad, the question was asked. His eyes filled with tears as he replied: 'No, sir; we were pals.' Such an incident will surely suffice to erase from the mind the false impression, which, unfortunately a few seem to have gathered, that the Australian is devoid of sentiment.

SUNDAY, 'SOMEWHERE IN FRANCE'

The question that leaps to the lips in connexion with the title of this chapter is, Why should the events associated with this particular day be recorded? Are they different from what takes place on any or all of the other days of the week—something special which clearly denotes that one week has ended and another week begun? Is there a temporary cessation of hostilities, during which bells are rung and men may be seen wending their way to some established building for worship, or does that indefinable stillness peculiar to the first day of the week in peaceful places pervade all life?

Apart from the interest and curiosity that many attach thereto, there is no significance in the selection of the day, and there is little if anything associated with the events of Sunday at the Front to distinguish it from any other day. Yet it is strange that though men may frequently confuse the days between Monday and Saturday, they instinctively seem to know when Sunday has come. Whether by chance or convenience, I know not, some of the biggest 'stunts' have been initiated on the Lord's Day. At times the voice of the Padre was scarcely heard above the din and noise of heavy guns as they dispatched their projectiles of destruction and death over the place in which a church parade was being conducted. The recollection of certain events and experiences of some Sundays will undoubtedly tend to make many a man more thoughtful and analytic than the events or experiences entered into on any other day during his active service career.

The disposition of an army is not affected by certain days, but by developments within the area of operations. If Sunday should be considered the opportune time for putting over a barrage, making a raid on the enemy lines, or effecting an advance, no thought of the sacred associations of that day is given serious consideration. The system in vogue provides for units when not in the line to be in reserve or resting. Such units supply working and carrying parties; so that the number of men available for church services on Sunday is no greater than on ordinary days. The war proceeds. Man may worship when opportunity permits.

A summary of the events of one Sunday will suffice to convey an idea of how almost every Sunday is spent at the Front. The weather is seasonable: over the country a dense mist hangs low in the early morn. The sun rises, and the mist flees before it, revealing the face of the earth covered with snow, mud, or in the tight grip of 'Jack Frost.' Aeroplanes glide gracefully overhead. They are out for observation purposes, or to prevent the approach of enemy craft. The artillery, ever alert both day and night, sends out its missiles of death far into the enemy's lines. The enemy guns reply, and thus it might continue through the day. Shells are ugly killers and wounders; but for them there would be little of the slaughter-yard suggestion about a modern battlefield, with its improved system of well-built and cleanly kept trenches and its clean puncturing bayonet thrust or rifle bullet. While the shells shriek and whirr through the air, heaps of humanity are distributed about the trenches, in the dug-outs, or in the reserve lines. The men sit or lie about for the most part, as unconcerned as if on holiday bent. The order to 'stand to' would bring them to their appointed places, from whence they would resist an invasion of their lines by the enemy, or launch an attack, make a raid, or go forth on patrol of 'no man's land.'

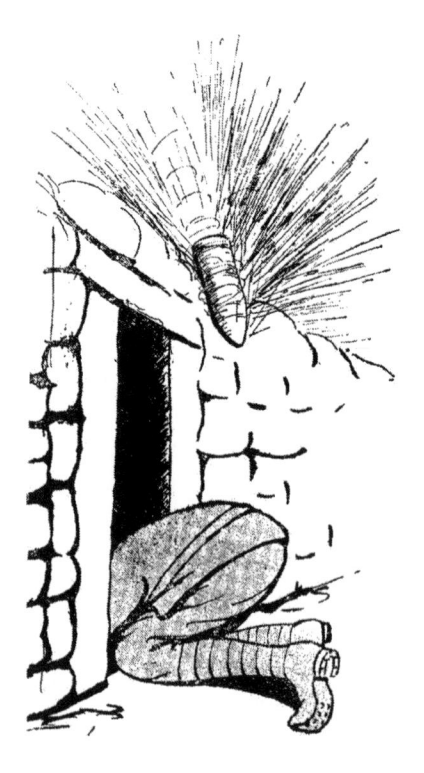

The Ostrich.
Back from the lines units are resting or engaged on the lines of

communication; from such units men are available for church parades. Men of different units and of different theological views come together in one place and worship God. Buildings are not always available for parade services. Sometimes they are held in the open field, in farm-yards, or in billets; frequently in tents provided by the Y.M.C.A. Attendance at these services is purely voluntary, and a large proportion of men attend whenever opportunity offers. While the service is in progress the war goes on. The men in the trenches catch the strains of band music, and there is carried over the distance intervening the sound of the singing of old familiar hymns. It is a privilege to speak to these men who have been in the shell-swept trenches, who have participated in raids, who have taken part in one of the most successful battles of the war, who have seen suffering and even looked into the face of death.

Several parades might be held during the day at hours convenient to those who wish to attend, and in the evening a song-service is conducted, when the men choose the hymns which they would sing. They are reverent in attitude, earnest in attention.

Sundays are no different from other days of the week. They merely mark, as do other days, the passing of time, which will bring either grief or gladness to those who watch and wait for the day of peace, and to us who war a victory crowned with honour. There is no *Sun*-day. The thick, dark cloud of war hides the sun's bright face, but there is hope in the thought that Sun-day is prophetic as well as historic, and insistently in its recurrence directs us to wait patiently for the cloud-bursts out of which shall emerge the Sun of Righteousness, who will proclaim such time to be the Day of the Lord.

For, lo, the days are hastening on
By prophet bard foretold,
When with the ever circling years
Comes round the age of gold.
When peace shall over all the earth
Its ancient splendours fling,
And all the world take up the song
Which angels once did sing:
'Glory to God in the highest, on earth
peace, goodwill toward men.'

SOLDIERS' SUPERSTITIONS

With the advent of Christmas, arrangements were effected by which officers whose work necessitated their being temporarily separated from the unit could come together for the purpose of observing the special season in the established epicurean style. Every effort was made to make the day as distinct from other days as circumstances would allow. Donations from the officers and small contributions from the men enabled those who had the matter in hand to provide the customary Christmas dinner. Though it was not served up on tables, spread with linen, and the usual impedimenta of the banqueting-table, it was greatly appreciated, and afforded a rare opportunity for reunion. Fresh friendships were formed, acquaintances renewed, brothers and relatives met after months of separation. Toasts were honoured and carols or hymns appropriate to the season were sung. A great deal had been heard or read about our troops fraternizing with the enemy during the Christmas seasons of the previous years of the war, but there was none of that during the Christmas of 1916. There was no cessation of hostilities. The lines were held with the same keenness, and there was considerable aerial and artillery activity throughout the day and night. In fact, Christmas 'Somewhere in France' was born to the accompaniment of the boom of guns and the whirr of aeroplanes. The weather conditions were decidedly inclement, and, despite the good wishes from friends in the Homeland, it was difficult to keep warm.

At the back of the lines, in a certain battalion's H.Q. billets, a number of officers had assembled. They had come together by invitation to participate in a reunion dinner. Everything had been done to make it a meal worthy of the occasion. Great taste had been displayed in decorating the table, and the cooks excelled themselves in the quality of the food served. We seated ourselves immediately 'Grace' was said, when somebody remarked that there were thirteen only, and suggested that another be asked in to make fourteen. Little notice was taken of the remark until the same officer ventured to predict that one of them would 'go out' before the year ended. He was teased with being unduly superstitious and attaching too much significance to the supposed unluckiness of the number thirteen. His mind was evidently depressed with the impression which he had gathered, and there was not lacking evidence that the gathering ceased to interest him further.

Despite the good wishes from friends in the Homeland, it was difficult to keep warm.

Exactly a week passed, and another such reunion had been arranged for the purpose of celebrating the passing of the old year and the ushering in of the new. Several jocularly remarked that for G———'s sake we should arrange to have more or less than thirteen present. Late on the afternoon of the last day of the year, advice was received at B.Q.H. that Lieut. G——— had been killed. He had gone down to the trenches to inspect some work which was being done by his platoon, and was on the point of returning when an enemy shell burst and a shrapnel bullet went through his heart. This sad event recalled to us his words at the gathering on Christmas night. His prediction that one would be missing ere the year ended was fulfilled, and he was the one called hence. Arrangements for the evening function were cancelled, and the next day his remains were interred in the military cemetery, and the grave is now marked by a beautiful cross made by a member of his platoon and inscribed by his O.C. He was a fine fellow, full of fun and life, a true comrade, an ideal officer, beloved by all who knew him.

The following pathetic incident speaks of the attachment which springs up between officers and men, and incidentally testifies to the high esteem in which our late comrade was held by one who had exceptional opportunities for knowing him. Duty took me to the cemetery a few days after the burial, and I noticed standing at the graveside with uncovered and bowed head a soldier of the battalion. I could see that the lad was deeply affected, and inquired as to whether he had known Lieut. G——. 'Yes sir,' he replied; 'I was his orderly; and—I miss him so much.'

Superstitions play a large part in the life of the average soldier, and frequently gain the ascendancy over common sense. Though rather reticent about expressing his religious views, he is in many respects intensely religious. He may admit being superstitious and even boast about it, or declare himself to be a fatalist. Fatalism in the vocabulary of the soldier is just another name for Providence.

Few, if any, are afraid of death. They seldom give it a thought. The general belief is that if a man's 'time' has come, nothing can possibly avert it. Under this impression he goes into battle or takes up his position in the lines. He consistently refuses, however, to be a party to anything which is considered at all likely to precipitate the end. For instance, no amount of persuasion would induce him to be one of three to receive a light for his cigarette or pipe from the same match, and owing to the strange coincidences in connexion with the number thirteen, he is prepared to deny himself much.

A silent tribute to the brave.

While soldiers are ever ready to avail themselves of every possible comfort when in the trenches, they hesitate to make use of a field service stretcher. They prefer to make their bed on the ground, under the impression that if they were to lie on stretchers in the trenches they would be carried out from the trenches on stretchers. One of a draft of reinforcements was attached to a platoon which had been detailed to proceed to the lines. On arrival, this man, despite many warnings from the others, took possession of a stretcher and used it as a bed. About eleven o'clock the following morning, the same stretcher was used to carry him back to the R.A.P. While working in the lines he was seriously wounded by a piece of shrapnel. It is hardly necessary to state that this man was completely won over to the belief which only the previous evening he had laughed at.

At the head of a trench in the vicinity of Ploegsteert a rusted revolver which had been found by a working party was suspended from a short pole. It caught the eye of all who passed by on their way up the lines. Nearly every man was seen to touch that useless weapon. Upon making enquiries it was ascertained that a superstition had grown up round that revolver. It was supposed to possess a certain charm, and the men who merely touched it on their way into the line would be protected from all danger. Certainly many incidents occurred which tended to support the belief that the mud covered rusted revolver possessed all the remarkable miraculous powers attributed to it.

In course of conversation with a soldier, I questioned the advisability of his proceeding to the trenches. 'Oh,' he declared, 'it is all right; no matter where I may be, if a shell has my number on it, I will have to take delivery, whether I like it or not.' While working in the lines a few days later a shell penetrated the parapet and buried its nose in the clay at the edge of the duck-boards. Allowing sufficient time to elapse to ascertain whether it was 'alive' (it proved to be a 'dud') he then examined the base of the shell, and was astonished to read thereon his regimental number.

Such coincidences tend to strengthen the superstitious tendencies of the soldier, and the effect upon most minds is to lead them to believe that a man's death or deliverance is absolutely due to Fate, which is just another way of saying, 'There's a Divinity which shapes our ends, rough hew them as we may.'

TO

THE WIDOWS

OF

FRANCE

ON THE EVE OF BATTLE

TO THE WIDOWS OF FRANCE

Eyes that have rained tears, lips that have trembled,
    Twitching convulsively, torn with their grief.
    Now face us bravely with pride undissembled,
    Glad to have suffered to show their belief.
    Troop upon troop of them, some walking singly,
    Weaker ones plodding in pairs for support;
    Mates to the spirits of men who were kingly,
    Coming from Matins with old men's escort.
    Ask them, ye watchers, inquire their elation,
    Tell them ye wonder they bear them so brave.
    Proudly they'll answer, 'La belle France, our nation,
    Requires us to suffer, our country to save.'
    To save from the maw of the great avaricious,
    The cold scheming brain of a commerce run mad—
    A commerce all-grasping and sordid and vicious;
    For this are we martyred, for this are we glad.
    Then the soul of the Springtime, the great resurrection,
    Shines bright in their faces, they wave to the car,
    Packed tight with our comrades, a cheery collection,
    As we dash thro' the streets to the trenches afar.
    And France comes to meet us, to cheer us and greet us,
    As we race past the fields to the woods brightly green,
    Whose young leaves half rustle with a great show of bustle
    When we halt at the fairest of spots ever seen.[1]
    Where the old kings of history, now shrouded in myst'ry,
    Once hunted the boar, or the feather, or fur.
    But we feel this is over as we wade thro' the clover,
    No tyrant again in this great wood shall stir.

For France now demands it; however she stands it,
However those brave ones in thousands can smile,
Requires some explaining, so cease all complaining,
And come on and battle and make it worth while.
Yes! on to the thunder, tho' it's a blunder,
On to the swish and the whine and the roar;
With the memoried face of one you called 'treasure,'
Above and around and ever before.
Oh! thou in that homeland so wistfully waiting,
Watching and wearing your worries or woe,
So proudly triumphant, consider such women;
Work for them, pray for them, smile as you go.
For into the furnace they've thrown all their 'treasures,'
Knowing that out of the vibrating whole,
Quiveringly molten, pulsating, gleaming,
Europe shall find her immaculate soul—
Soul of the suff'ring, bleeding and dying,
Soul of a freedom unselfish and clean,
Loving the light of a love all around us,
Scorning the actions of men who are mean.
Oh! men who were kingly, mated to martyrs
(Silently, cheerfully, plodding along),
Send all ye can of such great souls to help us,
Make us and keep us triumphant and strong.
G.P. Cuttriss and J.W. Hood.

FOOTNOTES:

[1] Ploegsteert.

'OVER THE TOP.'

From the time of our arrival in France until a week or two prior to the battle of Messines, general dissatisfaction was expressed by the troops because of the seeming slow progress that was being made. The men soon tired of the uneventful trench warfare. They were eager to go 'over the top.' Defensive operations did not appeal to them; they were impatient to assume the offensive. To put it in their own language, they had enlisted not to dig trenches or repair roads, but to fight the Hun. Certainly the monotony was relieved by an occasional raid, for which work they earned for the Division a splendid reputation. The area which the Division occupied was known throughout France as the 'Nursery,' where men, new to the modern mode of waging war, had opportunity for gaining experience and getting accustomed to shell and machine-gun fire under comparatively safe conditions.

During this period of 'marking time' the men were engaged both day and night on works of importance, without which an offensive would have meant sheer suicide. The elaborate preparations that were being made denoted that a big 'push' was contemplated. In connexion with this work, the pioneers and the engineers did magnificently.

Everything was arranged according to well-conceived plans, and the preliminaries to an unprecedented offensive were completed by June 6. Guns of different calibre were massed at points of vantage, cleverly camouflaged to conceal them from enemy observation. Dumps were replete with the necessary supplies of ammunition, and scrupulous regard was paid to arrangements for keeping the lines of communication clear. Provision was made for the treatment of wounded and their evacuation, and for the burial of the killed. Refreshment stalls were established at convenient points, where the attacking troops and the wounded could receive hot coffee and biscuits. Nothing that could be done for the comfort of the men and to ensure the success of the venture was overlooked.

Only those who are actually at the Front have any conception of the amount of work involved in assuming the aggressive. The staff responsible for perfecting the organization are deserving of the highest praise. There had been numerous rumours in connexion with mines. The air was electric, the men were confident, and all were determined to do their level best to uphold the splendid traditions bequeathed by older Australian units.

During the night preceding the dawn of June 6 the troops who were to take part in the attack marched to their respective assembling points. The march was uneventful up to a certain stage, after which large clouds of gas were encountered, which rendered necessary the wearing of respirators. Despite the sickly sensation produced by the inhalation of gas, the troops advanced. There is much to be written of the latter part of the approach march, but that will be recorded by others. It is sufficient to state that certain unforeseen events threatened to seriously disorganize things, but these were overcome as they were met with.

Almost simultaneously with the first faint streak of the dawn of June 7 the mines at Hill 60 and St. Yves were exploded. The sight was awe-inspiring, and the ground trembled as if in the throes of an agonizing palsy. On the tick of the appointed time our 'boys' went 'over the top.' It was for this experience that they had worked and waited. They advanced immediately behind the barrage so consistently sustained by the artillery, and in the face of a terrific fusilade of machine-gun fire which seemed to leap upon them from almost every angle. Some of the enemy machine-guns were captured by our troops, who used them with deadly effect upon the then retiring foe. All the objectives were obtained with clock-like precision. Again and again the victorious troops were subjected to withering counter-attacks, and shells fell around them like hail. There was no faltering. They held the recovered ground in the face of a merciless tornado of steel and bullets.

As the infantry advanced, the pioneers and engineers followed, digging trenches, extending tramways, and keeping the lines of communication clear. No pen, however facile, could give the true lines to the picture. Ordinary language is inadequate to express all that was achieved, seen, and felt. The men did splendidly. The respective work of the several services was perfectly co-ordinated, so much so that after the 'stunt' it seemed as if a mutual admiration society had been spontaneously organized. The infantry congratulated the Flying Corps, the Flying Corps complimented the Artillery, and both Artillery and Flying Corps were loud in their praise of the dauntless Infantry. All did their part, and the taking of Messines will probably be chronicled as one of the greatest, if not the greatest, of battles in connexion with this world-war.

Prior to this engagement the Third Division had experienced but a sprinkling of fire, but during its progress it received its baptism, and emerged from the battle with a reputation of which any unit might be proud. It was a stupendous task, a severe test for the 'baby' Division, but every man rose to the occasion. The wounded were cheerful, the dead died gloriously, and those of us who are alive and remain are proud to have had some part in such an important and eminently successful undertaking.

There were many acts of heroism, some of which have been officially recognized. The Australians have the utmost contempt for the enemy as fighting men. They declare that if the artillery and air-craft were eliminated they would be prepared to give the enemy the benefit of odds in hand-to-hand fighting.

One instance will suffice to illustrate their indomitable spirit. While the 'push' was in progress, a man who, in his own words, had 'stopped one,' was carried to an R.A.P. His wounds were numerous and rather serious. Two fingers of the left hand had been blown off, his right arm was shattered, his head and neck were much cut about, and blood oozed from wounds on his chest. This man had got a 'Blighty,' but he did not appear to be at all pleased. It should be stated that the men who receive wounds sufficiently serious to warrant their being sent to hospitals in England are considered, and consider themselves, very fortunate. He was disappointed because he was wounded, not that he complained about his disfigurement or the pain. I expressed my sympathy and wished him a speedy recovery and a happy time in 'Blighty,' and suggested that possibly there would be no need for him to return, for the Hun might soon be driven out from Belgium. He eyed me unflinchingly, and endeavoured to raise himself on his uninjured elbow, and then blurted out, 'It is just as well for the —— Huns that I got wounded.' These were not the exact words he used. There were many accompanying adjectives, without which the vocabulary of the Australian would be very limited indeed. This big-hearted, whole-souled, hefty 'Westralian' seemed to think that the issue to that particular 'push' depended absolutely upon him.

The men of the Third Division have now had the experience which many had longed for. Going 'over the top' was not quite so romantic as fancy had pictured it to be, and the experience which is common to all who take part in it for the first time defies expression. A peculiar sensation creeps annoyingly slowly along the spinal column, subtly affecting every member of the body. There's a gripping of the heart and a numbing of the brain, and the tongue persistently cleaves to the roof of the mouth, which seems as dry as powdered chalk. A choking sensation accompanies every effort to cough. You may be in the stepping-off trench or lying face-down on the churned-up mud out on 'no man's land,' waiting for the signal to 'go.' The seconds tick slowly by, the minutes are leaden-footed in their passing, and seem like eternities.

The eyes are almost blinded through the strain of peering into darkness, the imagination runs riot, grotesque shapes are conjured into view, only to be dissipated by a solitary flare or a series of gun-flashes. The fact that it is raining and you are lying in a gradually deepening pool of water occasions no concern. What matters most is that your puttees are frayed or your boots in need of repair, but you console yourself with the thought that after the 'stunt' it will be easy to get a new outfit, and maybe you commence to make plans as to how you will spend your leave. You appear to be quite oblivious to the fact that the next moment may be your last.

Ages roll by; suddenly you are conscious of somebody by your side; you make an attempt to smile, when at the same instant the ground trembles as if in the throes of a tremendous earthquake; flash after flash in quick succession; the air vibrates with noises that deafen; hundreds of shells hurtle overhead. 'That's 'er,' shouts the man by your side. You are pleased that something has happened to divert your mind from its morbid fancyings. This is the 'Dinkum.' The electrical effect upon your mind and body is wonderful. You break from the shackles that fear and fancy have thrown round you. The reports of terrific explosions rend the air, you grip frantically at the soft mud to prevent yourself being hurled through space. Somebody from somewhere makes a sign, and in a moment you are erect and speeding in the direction of the enemy lines. There is but one thought in the mind as you allow your hand to tighten round your rifle—to gain your objective. Heaven help the Hun who attempts to frustrate you. 'Hurrah!' The wire has been smashed to smithereens, and in less time than it takes to describe you are 'over the top'— close up to the enemy line. You stumble forward, onward, without noticing the broken nature of the ground. The sight of the enemy rushing towards you with hands well above their heads, shouting 'Kamerad,' or fleeing before your advance, excites greater enthusiasm.

You begin to notice other things. Possibly the first thing that dawns upon your mind is that others are taking part in the business—that you are not alone. Then you notice the effect of our shell-fire; this inspires greater confidence, and involuntarily you thank heaven for such splendid artillery. Then you notice little heaps clad in familiar khaki—they are what remain of comrades who have sealed their love of country with their blood. You observe others wandering aimlessly about, suffering from shell-shock; or the gallant stretcher-bearers, regardless of all danger, attending to the wounded and carrying them back for treatment. The sight does not grieve or shock you—only surprise is evinced by a change in facial expression. You just carry on—the shock and grief will come later. You just grit your teeth and take a fresh grip of your rifle and go forward with greater determination to strike a blow in the cause of freedom and honour. Maybe you reach your objective, your clothes sodden with sticky, clammy mud and possibly the red of your own blood showing through.

The whole thing has been like some dream of adventure with wild beasts;

but there is firmly embedded in your consciousness the knowledge that you have done the job. Other waves of men pass through the line which you have wrested from the Hun; you cheer them as they pass, and then dig in for all you are worth.

A few days later there appears in the daily papers, under the heading of 'British Official,' that the troops penetrated the enemy's lines to such and such a depth, and have bravely withstood several terrific counter-attacks; and war correspondents will cable the news to our waiting people of the Homeland that the 'boys' magnificently stormed and won additional fame; but if you want it in the every-day language of the man from 'down under,' he merely went 'over the top.'

After the rush there is no time for rest. The recovered ground must be retained. New positions have to be consolidated, fresh gun positions have to be constructed. The lines must be made habitable. The dead have to be buried. The efficient and expeditious manner in which this work was accomplished established the Third Division's right to full participation in the honour and glory of the taking and holding of Messines by the Second Anzacs.

SHELLS: A FEW SMILES AND A CONTRAST

When the guns begin to speak, and shells are hurtling through the air, places of shelter are resorted to. These places are not always shell-proof, but they serve as a protection against splinters. There are few places that would withstand the effects of a direct hit by a heavy shell, but one feels perfectly safe with even a sheet of iron overhead. The effects of an explosion are very local, and the chances of a direct hit are very remote. The first law of nature takes precedence during a bombardment. Precaution is esteemed to be much better than a blanket and burial.

In and about the towns at the back of the lines where the troops are billeted there are a sprinkling of civilians. When these places are being shelled they display no fear. Occasionally elderly people will cover their heads with their hands and seek shelter in the cellars, while the soldier, ostrich-like, is quite contented provided he has some protection for his head, but the majority continue with their work as in normal times. When the civilians were questioned as to whether they were afraid of the enemy breaking through and carrying them off or killing them, they would confidently reply, 'Oh, no! British between.' They feel perfectly safe, knowing that the British are between them and the Hun.

Many of them have good reason to remember the time when the enemy were in occupation of the town. In some instances the Germans have been highly spoken of. I give credence to every good report. Personally, we bear them no ill-will. We detest the system which has made them what they are, and we are here to crush it, and sincerely hope that the men of the German race who, however, mistaken, are ready to lay down their lives for their country, may emerge from this war and be re-made on the anvil of defeat, and in the days to be redeem to honour the name which to-day is the synonym for all that is brutal and abhorrent.

That all of them are not filled with implacable hatred towards the British is evidenced in the following incident. We attempted to raid the enemy trenches. The weather was bitterly cold and the night was dark. Our artillery put over a heavy barrage, after which the raiding party went forth; they crept forward over the muddy ground, and entered the German lines. Several casualties were sustained during the operations. When our men returned to their trenches, it was discovered that one of the raiding party was missing. When the noise of the counter-barrage had died down, a cry for help was distinctly heard by our front line troops. It came from 'no man's land.' A couple of stretcher-bearers and two men went out in search of the one in distress. While groping about amongst the wire in the darkness, they heard the Germans assuring the man for whom they were searching that he would be all right. Suddenly the enemy turned a trench searchlight on to 'no man's land,' and by this light the search party were guided to their wounded comrade. The light was kept on him until he was rescued, and was then used to guide the party back to their own lines. During this time no shot was fired. This was a humane action indeed.

All the Huns, however, are not so humanely disposed. In connexion with another raid on the enemy trenches, our men met with violent opposition, but succeeded in obtaining their objective. When returning, a few of the party were wounded—one very seriously. He was unable to make his way back. The Germans got him, stripped him of his uniform, and left him against the wire. The weather being intensely cold, the man soon died from exposure. These two incidents illustrate the two extremes in the attitude of the Huns towards the British. One was a brutal act of hatred, the other a humane act, which commends itself to both friend and foe.

To see ourselves as others see us.

The Germans have been credited with almost every conceivable atrocity that man is capable of perpetrating. Whether these brutalities are perpetrated with the sanction of the German authorities, or are merely the expression of individual hatred, one is not prepared to state. We have ceased to be angry with or alarmed at their tactics of intimidation. We interpret every act of frightfulness as evidence of desperate conditions. The only effect that such devilish methods have upon the men in the lines is to make them more determined to crush the mad and murderous spirit of militarism which holds the Hun in its merciless grip.

During ordinary trench warfare the enemy appears to concentrate his artillery fire on to the towns and villages at the back of our lines. Villages have been practically eliminated and large towns reduced to a heap of ruins. The destruction of these places is of no military consequence. It is pure vandalism.

50   SHELLS: A FEW SMILES AND A CONTRAST

With the aid of electric torches ... we descended to the cellar.

Bairnsfather's sketches portraying the humour and coolness that such critical conditions create are in no particular exaggerated. A certain building, prominently situated in a fairly large town, within easy range of the enemy guns, was being used as B.H.Qs. It afforded accommodation for about twelve officers and as many other ranks. The outskirts of the town had been subjected to severe shelling during the day. Towards evening the shelling ceased, but commenced again about midnight; on this occasion the shells were directed more to the centre of the town. Pieces of iron and a hail of shrapnel descended upon the roof of our billet. All were awakened by the noise. From different parts of the building the same query was advanced: 'Are you all right?' Then a hurried conference was held, and the C.O. decided that discretion was the better part of valour. With the aid of electric torches we collected our blankets, etc., and descended to the cellar. Everybody was cheerful. The report of the guns somewhere along the enemy's lines was heard distinctly, and we would wait for the swish of the shells as they hurtled through the air. Almost simultaneously with the swish would come the crash followed by the sound of breaking glass and falling bricks, and involuntarily we exclaimed in chorus, 'Another one in.' We thought of the poor devils who may have been in the vicinity where the shell exploded, and various expressions of sympathy escaped from our lips. Almost immediately on reaching the cellar, there was a terrific explosion, and one of the chimneys of the building crashed into the cellar. Gradually we lost interest and became almost indifferent to what was going on. One by one we repaired to our improvised beds on the floor. Sometimes one would have difficulty in wooing the goddess of sleep, and his persistency in asking questions was exceeded only by the annoyance experienced by those to whom the questions were addressed. The usual question of the sleepless individual is 'Where did that one land?' and the answer with some accompanying adjectives is invariably, 'I am more concerned about where the next one will land.'

The enemy generally commences shelling these places at the close of day, and the men have described these operations as 'The Hun's evening hate.' On one occasion a certain village was being strafed. Several men of a certain battalion were on the road at the time. They quickly availed themselves of the shelter of a cellar. The building was hit several times. Shortly after the bombardment commenced a man leading a mule was observed, coming along the road. He was invited to take shelter in the cellar. The invitation was accepted with alacrity. The mule was tethered to the window-sill, and the man was soon in their midst. Shells continued to burst overhead and round about. The newcomer proved to be a blessing. He soon had the men laughing despite the noise and danger. When a shell burst in close proximity to the building, he evinced great concern for the safety of his mule. 'My poor old "donk,"' he would exclaim; 'there goes his tail.' Another burst: 'There goes his hind-quarters.' It seemed impossible for the mule to escape injury or death. Turning to his companions he declared that he would carry part of that mule back. If his head were left intact he would gather the harness and wrap it round the head and carry it back to the lines, and if the O.C. transport asked where the 'donk' was, he would say, 'Shot from under me, sir.' Suddenly the shelling ceased, and they emerged from their shelter. The mule's master was the first outside. He fully expected to see but a blood-stain on the spot where he had left the beast, but to his great surprise and satisfaction he saw the mule serenely nibbling at the grass growing alongside the building. The old 'donk' had not sustained an injury. To say that he was proud to lead a whole mule back to his quarters instead of having to carry only its head, is an altogether inadequate way of describing his actual feelings.

'Did you hear that one, Bill?'

'Did you hear that one, Bill?' asked one man of another who had come along the shell-swept road rather hurriedly.

'Yes,' replied the nearly exhausted man, 'I heard it twice; once when it passed me, and again when I passed it.'

MESSINES

JUNE 7, 1917

A shell-struck souvenir of hellish war,
    A monument of man's stupendous hate!
    Can this have been a Paradise before,
    Now up-blown, blasted, drear and desolate?
    Aye, once with smiling and contented face
    She reigned a queen above a charming place.
    But soon the sport of leaders and of kings
    Transformed her to a resting-place for guns,
    Rude scars across her breasts the worker flings,
    To shelter countless hordes of hell-born Huns,
    The while, upon the next opposing crest,
    Our men died gamely as they did their best.
    And thus for years, with cold, relentless zeal,
    With fiendish science both sides fought and watched,
    From loop-holes or from clouds which half conceal,
    Or in deep tunnels all their skill was matched.
    On sentry in the firebay, or the hov'ring 'plane,
    Mining and countermining yet again.
    And far behind such scenes, great engineers
    Pondered o'er problems without parallel.
    And planned with wisdom of a thousand years,
    To blow the other to eternal Hell.
    Their calculations left no callous scheme untried,
    To slaughter hundreds of the other side.
    But hush! the whole machinery's complete,
    All plans are folded and the great work's done,
    The work of building up to cause defeat—
    The lever's pulled, and, lo! a new work has begun.
    The task of falling on a shattered foe,
    And doing things undreamed-of years ago.

Hush! hark! A mighty rumbling roar breaks thro',
And see! Her crest-line leaps into a flame,
The foul disease within her bowels she blew
High into the air to rid her of her shame;
In one huge vomit she now flings her filth,
Far o'er the country in a powdered 'tilth.'
And so the vassals of a fiendish foe
Are scattered far and wide into a dust.
Those who have revelled as they wreaked red woe,
A shattered sample of their own blood-lust.
Whilst from our hill-crest and its catacomb,
A new life comes a-pouring from the tomb.
Eager, and burning with the zeal of youth,
Our Second Anzacs sprang from out the ground,
Bound by their mateships and their love of truth,
The Third Division its new soul has found;
Straight o'er the top amidst a hail of shell
To their objective which they knew so well.
On, on, thro' poison gas and rattling roar,
Past ulc'rous craters, blackened foul and deep,
These comrades 'stuck' as ne'er they had before.
And kept together in their rushing sweep;
Deafened and rattled, hung up in the wire,
Helping each other thro' such fearful fire.
On still until they reached the furthest goal,
There to dig in and hold the new-won line.
By linking up each torn and shattered hole—
By no means easy, but their grit was fine—
They fought and worked like demons till the dawn,
Harried and pestered by the 'Kaiser's spawn.'
And, baffled from his gun-pits far away,
Low-down, well south, an angry foe doth roar,
He opens out again upon another day
And rakes the slope with shrapnel as before.
But only working parties on the top are found,
The rest, save A.M.C., are underground.
Strange sights are seen upon that battle-ground,
But stranger still are unearthed from below;
Here many supermen may now be found,
Just watch those stretcher-bearers where *they* go,
And see those parties bearing food and drink,
Past all those blizzard shells—then stand and think!
But one poor shell-crazed loon roamed far and wide;
Sweat-grimed, wild-eyed, and now bereft of all.

'Me mates? W'ere is my mates?' he plaintive cried,
'They's in that 'ole with me when it did fall.'
We took him to three huddled heaps near by,
But he roamed on as tho' he wished to die.
And as the sun's great light bursts o'er the scene,
La Petit Douve, one-time a sparkling stream,
Now sluggish slides, red-tinted, she has been
Past horrors thro' the night and *did not dream*.
For many days she'll, silent, strive to bear
Such human wreckage down a path once fair.
G.P. Cuttriss and J.W. Hood.

The illustrator feeling happy, yet looking 'board.'

Bill the Bugler

BILL THE BUGLER

I well remember when the subject of this sketch 'joined up.' He was small of stature, and his general appearance was by no means prepossessing. That he had seen a good deal of the world was very evident, even to the most superficial observer. His language was picturesque, though not profane. A few weeks sufficed to 'lick him into shape,' and he presented a fairly tolerable figure in uniform. At spinning yarns he was an adept, and at camp concerts could invariably be depended upon for an item or two, always of a humorous nature.

Bill quickly established himself amongst the 'boys' as a general favourite. This enviable position he still occupies. On account of his duties as bugler requiring him to be one of the first up in the morning, and one of the last to retire at night, he sought a change of duty. He became a bandsman, then a stretcher-bearer, and eventually was detailed to assist in a cook-house—in cook-house terminology an 'off-sider.'

Though Bill had as much military experience as most of us, we could not think of him as a soldier. That our opinion of him was justified the following incident will illustrate. A party of officers, including a staff-major, was inspecting cooking and billeting arrangements in our quarters. Bill, who happened to have a couple of hours off that day, was strolling towards the party. He was in cook-house attire—tunicless, his hat well back on his head, shirt-sleeves rolled to the elbow, hands deep in his breeches pockets, a cigarette between his lips. Regardless of the critical eyes which were focused upon him, he sauntered leisurely towards the officers, and when in line with them he nodded and said 'Good-day.' The officers stopped, and one of them peremptorily inquired, 'Aren't you a soldier?' 'Oh, no,' he replied; 'I'm D Company's cook!' His reply so amused the officers that he was allowed to continue on his way without being reminded that as a soldier he was required to salute all officers.

After spending a few weeks in the cook-house, he asked permission to go to the trenches when the battalion went into the line. The transfer was effected, and he made a start with real soldiering. No amount of discipline could transform him from the free-from-care, do-as-you-please individual into the polished soldier. One evening he was posted over the gas-alert in the front line trenches, when a shell exploded a few yards in front of him. The explosion caused his hat to disappear and the concussion projected him into a dug-out. Only the solidity of the wall prevented him from going further; as it was, the force with which he was hurled against the side of the dug-out made a deep impression on the damp wall. He lay in a motionless heap in the corner of the dug-out. A N.C.O. rushed along the duck-boards, thrust his head into the dug-out, and anxiously inquired of Bill as to whether he was hurt. Bill by this time had partially recovered from the shock. His small steel-grey eyes gradually opened. The N.C.O. again asked if he were hurt. Bill's eyes rolled, his lips moved, and then he blurted out, 'Oh, no, only my feelings!'

Bill is not a man to make a fuss about anything. He has no time for red-tape in any shape or form, it is true, but whatever work is assigned him is always done satisfactorily. Whether he is any less a soldier or his efficiency as a fighting force impaired because of his failure to meet the rigid requirements of an exacting military regulation is a matter concerning which there might be a difference of opinion; but this at least stands to his credit: he knows no fear, is the life of the unit, and the battalion to which he belongs would sustain a distinct loss by the removal of Bugler Bill, &c.

A TRAGEDY OF THE WAR

From strife they now march back to smiling farms,
    Recoiling from the crash and smoke and roar.
    Meadows, all verdant, faerie fields, whose charms
    Serve for a space to make them as before.
    And peaceful pictures of the days of yore,
    With thrilling thoughts of those they left behind
    Flash thro' the mental vision, and a score
    Of letters brightly occupy the mind
    Without a care, or woe, or doubt of any kind.
    Anon they journey from this place of rest
    By night or early dawn back to the brink
    Of that volcanic crater where the best
    Sit tight, scarce caring if they swim or sink.
    Silent they bear it, as they quietly think
    The end approaching to their life at last,
    And face each other, with a smile or wink
    Outwardly stoic, tho' their hearts beat fast
    As, thumping down, great shells come racing in and past.
    Erase such thoughts from out the o'er-wrought brain,
    Think rather of this freshness, and the sight
    Of nature in her harvest dress, refrain
    From plunging into the eternal night.
    Such contrasts seem the only choice by right
    Of those who battle for the joy of life.
    Out on this troubled spot where Armies fight,
    And peasants labour just behind such strife
    Shorthandedly, unhelped, save by a child or wife.
    So come with me down hedgerows, down the glades,
    And thro' the cosy glens, till far away
    We come unto a hill-crest—lights and shades,

Bright coloured landscapes far below us lay,
Blue mists and fields of yellow corn and hay,
In rows like soldiers, now the tired eyes see,
And poplars guard the distant dim roadway,
Whilst near the wind sighs thro' the acorn-tree,
Till one feels hushed, serene, contented, almost free.
And here, tucked back behind a leafy lane,
Low in a pocket of some sheltered ground,
An unpretentious farm, so snug and plain,
An invitation in itself; when found,
Only a whining howl like dingoes' sound,
Reminds one that there is a war near by.
The tools of peace see littered here around,
Weapons by which men learn to live, not die:
A plough, a drill, and there a binder standing nigh.
'*Bon jour, m'sieurs,*' a little hunchback cries;
A wizened, twisted human form divine;
She flashed a look of welcome from her eyes,
From which the soul of ages seem to shine.
'*Entrez,*' she welcomed, and her face looked fine,
As proudly bustling o'er her clean stone floor
She bade us linger, eat, and drink her wine.
Refreshed with food and drink, we loiter more
Within such cool retreat, delaying '*Au revoir.*'
And soon the human tragedy in course
Of progress thro' that little home becomes
Clear to the senses, and to us much worse
Compared with our Australia's peaceful homes.
For, oh, the pity, as one's vision roams
From there to here, and back on wings again;
A rush of feeling and emotion comes,
Whilst hearing this contorted piece of pain,
The stirring times of all their troubled lives explain.
For she to whom Fate seemed at first unkind,
Now lives an angel in a higher sphere.
This pained and twisted cripple seemed to find
Pleasure in living for her kinsfolk dear.
Hard work an honour, in her duty clear
To wives of brothers in the fighting line;
Women and children gather round her here;
For round their hearts her nature did entwine,
Her beaming face proclaimed 'See, Anglaise, they are mine.'
And all around these chubby children play,
Dirty, but happy, fed and cared for well,

A TRAGEDY OF THE WAR

With ne'er a troubled thought the live-long day,
For they know little of adjacent hell.
The hunchback warns us we are not to tell
About the 'Allemagne' whilst they are nigh,
Since all have known him in the past too well.
'Let them forget it as we often try.
C'est la guerre,' she said, and quickly brushed her eye.
And then she whispers, as we loiter near,
The story of their young lives years ago,
When, snatched from cradles, with a frenzied fear,
Their mothers hurried on before the foe;
Their men defend and screen them as they go,
And fight a rearguard action with the brute,
Who cares not for their agony or woe,
But only for the blood-streams and the loot.
And now she sees us watching one poor little mute:
'Ah! this one?' and she pointed to the dot
Who sat alone, and smiled to vacant space,
'Waits for her mother; very hard her lot;
For years now has she waited in her place.
"Where is her mother?" I can never trace
Somewhere beyond across "the no man's way."
Some day, perhaps,' she cried, with yearning face.
The tiny mite, tho' happy, could not play,
Except with little restless hands all day.
'Sometimes the shell come here right by,' she said.
'The other day, when I what you call wash,
A big boom quickly pass above my head,
And fall out in the field with a big crash.
But, oh, those children, they so very rash,
They know so little of the dreadful doom.
I come in time to save a fearful crash,
And catch them with the nose-cap in this room—
The nose-cap, unexhausted, from the boom.'
And then we start, inclined to say farewell.
We try to brighten up the little maid
Who sits alone, perhaps in faerie dell;
For she doth seem not in the least afraid.
She, smiling, takes the pennies which we lay
Within her hands, tho' distant is her smile;
And for a space she seemed with them to play,
But drops them ere we're scarcely gone, awhile
We wander back, half dumb, hard, thinking for a mile.

G.P. Cuttriss and J.W. Hood.

"She, smiling, takes the pennies which we lay
Within her hands...."

RECREATION BEHIND THE LINES

The Horse Show

The military authorities have ever recognized the importance and value of recreation in connexion with the training of men. They realize that 'all work and no play makes Tommy a dull boy'; and the provision that has been made for recreation and amusement for the 'boys' commands the deepest appreciation of both rank and file. The Australian is unaccustomed to the rigid restrictions of an inflexible military régime, and a temporary relaxation contributes much towards eliminating that feeling of 'fed-upness' to which he is so susceptible under monotonous and trying conditions, and certainly assists in making him a less dissatisfied soldier.

The sporting instinct is so ingrained in the average Australian that amusement and athletics have become part and parcel of his life, and his efficiency as a fighting force has been increased in consequence. His well-knit, muscular frame, and cheerful, free-from-care disposition, and love for clean sport, have won for him a place in the estimation of those who know and understand him, which is the envy of many. Australia has given to the world champions in almost every branch of sport, and the traditions which have been established on the football and cricket fields and in athletic circles in years preceding the war are being upheld and added to by her sons 'somewhere in France.'

A General's task is by no means an easy one. He has to safeguard against dissatisfaction, which invariably is the primary cause of breaches of discipline.

He requires to be tactful in the handling of his command, gain the confidence of the men, and enlist their undivided support; yet every consideration must be subordinate to the supreme task of winning the war. His methods must be such as will exact prompt obedience and beget respect, without imposing undue hardships and punishment.

The Third Division is exceedingly fortunate in having Major-General John Monash, C.B., V.D., in command. He is a popular and painstaking officer, a born leader, a strict disciplinarian, possessed of tireless energy. He has not spared himself in his efforts to establish and maintain a high standard of efficiency amongst all ranks. The G.O.C. set himself to put his men right and succeeded. He has a wonderfully comprehensive grip over every branch of activity, and woe betide the officer or man who is indifferent to or negligent of the duties entrusted to him. Any proposition calculated to benefit the men has always been favourably considered, and he has frequently been an interested spectator of various games that have been played just behind the lines. As a result there is little if any disaffection among the men of the Division. Major-General Monash has encouraged by approval and assistance various forms of recreation and entertainment. The splendid fighting record of the Third speaks eloquently of his capable leadership and the rousing and prolonged cheering which greets him when presiding over or addressing an assembly of his men leaves no doubt in the mind as to his popularity.

Off to the Horse Show.

For a few months after our arrival in France, a cinema afforded nightly entertainment. It was well patronized by the troops. The building used had seating accommodation for about seven hundred, and generally long before the hour of opening a queue of soldiers would assemble. There was no pushing or scrambling for tickets. The Australian good-humouredly submitted to the queue system, and patiently waited his turn. Mr. Frank Beaurepeare, of swimming fame, successfully managed the picture show, and eventually got together a few vocalists and comedians, who were organized into a pierrot group. These men were relieved from other duties during the comparatively quiet periods. Eventually a couple of talented Tommies were added to the group, which came to be designated the Coo-ees, under the direction of Mr. Dixon, the capable and energetic successor to Mr. F.B. Beaurepeare. In addition to performing every evening, the Coo-ees frequently gave out-door concerts during the day or in the men's billets, after the evening entertainment. A nominal charge for admission was made, and the proceeds were used to augment the Divisional Funds, which are used for the benefit of the men. These entertainments were given within easy range of the enemy guns. On several occasions shells fell in the vicinity of the hall, but few casualties were reported.

> 'Sweet and Low' by the quartette party always brought forth rounds of applause. - 'Try it a little softer.' Taff Williams, Musical Director

> Costumes were procured, and the programmes submitted were highly creditable and greatly appreciated. The quartette party was exceedingly popular, and never failed to please the 'boys.'

In addition to affording amusement, the Coo-ees did invaluable work during engagements. They either acted as stretcher-bearers or dispensed refreshments to the troops as they went forward to or returned from the trenches. They were located at dressing-stations or at R.A.P.'s. It is generally hoped that the party as at present constituted will be available after the war for the purpose of giving entertainments in Australia such as they gave to the tired war-hardened troops 'somewhere in France.'

Periodically horse shows and sports were arranged by D.H.Q. Substantial prizes and valuable trophies were awarded the successful competitors. The day's proceedings would be enlivened by band music. Impersonations of the world's mirth maker, Charlie Chaplin, and Australian 'sun-downers,' were decidedly clever and afforded much amusement. Horse shows always attract large attendances, and any vehicle going in the direction of the show grounds was practically commandeered by the tired but interested troops. They have a partiality, however, for 'M.T.' lorries. For weeks prior to the event, men would spend every available minute polishing chains, cleaning harness, painting vehicles, and grooming horses. Every unit has its admirers and supporters, and all events were keenly contested.

Sir Douglas Haig, G.C.B., G.C.V.O., and Sir A.J. Godley, K.C.B., K.C.M.G., at the 2nd Anzac Horse Show.

In addition to horse shows and sports organized by D.H.Q., the brigades and battalions within the Division arrange for fête days whenever opportunity offers. The manner in which these are carried out reflects the highest credit upon those responsible for their organization, and they have materially helped to bring about a better understanding between officers and men. Games appropriate to the season are played at the back of the lines. The ground selected for football or cricket may be shell-marked, and the materials used roughly made and incomplete. Football matches between different units have been as keenly contested on the muddy and broken fields of Belgium and France as those that have been played on the specially prepared grounds of the Homeland. The Australians have held their own against other units in both cricket and football.

For those who find such games too strenuous, indoor games are provided by the Australian Comforts Fund, the Y.M.C.A., or the League of Loyal Women of Australia. A circulating library is usually connected with the Y.M.C.A. or Church Army huts, so that practically every taste is catered for. An institution is justified in its existence by what it produces. Judged according to this canon, the various organizations which cater for the amusement and recreation of our fighting men have infallibly demonstrated their right to be, and should command the practical support of all who are interested in the well-being of our fighting men.

FOR THE CAUSE OF THE EMPIRE

Irrespective of the state which sent us forth, and despite our denominational and political differences, we are undivided in our admiration of those who, in the enthusiasm of deathless devotion, have made the supreme sacrifice for King and country. Words are inadequate to express the tribute which we would pay to the memory of our brave dead. We are beginning to value heroism more truly, and have not been blind to the valour of those who have fallen in the effort to uphold the honour and flag of the Empire. The story of their deeds makes the heart beat faster. Many have discovered that the most glorious use to which life could be put was to give it away. When the smoke has lifted and the noise died down, the confession made and the true history of this war written, then we shall see their heroism in the right light, and more fully appreciate their sacrifice in the interests of justice and honour. It matters not where they died—in hospital, on troopship, or on the battlefield; their presence in the Army was sufficient evidence of their willingness to bear their share of the cost in sacrifice that had to be made before the end could be achieved. They died as few men get the opportunity to die, fighting for all that is most worth while—for God, and right, and liberty—which is just another way of stating that they gave their lives for the glorious cause of the Empire.

The general impression is that the Empire consists of an aggregation of people, in possession of vast territories and enormous wealth: that it consists of Great Britain, Canada, India, South Africa, Australia, New Zealand, &c. Many cannot think of the Empire but in terms of territory, money, and men. The British Empire, like the Kingdom of God, is invisible. These material things are but the practical expression of great forces and unalterable principles such as freedom, democracy, justice, and faith, which lie at the very base of our national life. It is for the retention and general enjoyment of these things that we are fighting. We are not fighting for France, Belgium, nor even for the Empire, as it is generally regarded, but for the enforcement of those standards of justice and honour which have made us the greatest nation in the world. It is not a war of retaliation nor aggression, but a war to redress wrong, to succour the weak and down-trodden.

There is not lacking evidence that beneath the material aspects of this conflict there is a tremendous spiritual battle in progress, the issue of which will determine the value of these national assets. We cannot think that our comrades have given their lives merely to enlarge our borders or to increase our wealth. They have died for the cause of the Empire, and the cause of the Empire is synonymous with the cause of humanity, democracy, freedom, civilization—of Christianity.

The cause of the Empire is the cause of God. The highest standard of civilization finds expression in the readiness to make sacrifice that others might benefit. This standard has been splendidly exemplified by the 'boys' from Australia. This is the standard of the Empire as against that of Kultur, which is the suppression of the weak, the slaughter of the innocent, and the elimination of the small. The sacrifice has certainly been considerable, the price involved very great, but not too great. We are prepared to pay even a higher price rather than lose our heritage or forfeit our right to the enjoyment of the priceless privileges of freedom and justice. We cannot help the dead, but we can honour them, and we can best honour them by taking up the arms which they have laid down, filling the gaps which their death has made, and resting not until peace with honour shall have been established on firm and enduring foundations.

War is certainly an ugly business; it is hell; but better by far than the loss of liberty and civilization under the heel of Prussian militarism; and we would pay our humble tribute to the memory of our brave comrades who have freely given their lives for the cause of the Empire.

To those who have lost—the wives, mothers, and sweethearts—we extend our deepest sympathy, and trust that their deep sorrow will be tinged with pride in the knowledge that their dear ones died the noblest death that men may die.

OUR HEROIC DEAD

Our heroic dead, though war hath laid you low,
    And cruelly robbed you of this earthly life,
    You did your best against the fiendish foe,
    And gave your all to put an end to strife.
    Our comrades still, sleep on; your names will live
    Long after this terrific war hath ceased.
    No cannon's roar, no hurtling shell, no bomb
    Can harm thee or disturb your long last sleep.
    Down in your soldiers' graves you rest from toil,
    Without the knowledge of the Hun's fierce hate.
    The shell-struck, blood-stained clods of Belgian soil
    Will open to your souls the Pearly Gate.
    There is no place on this earth's troubled face
    So sacred as the ground which shields your heads,
    Fit resting-place for those so true and brave,
    Who for the cause the fullest price have paid.
    Australia's sons the sacrifice supreme
    For honour, truth, and freedom gladly made;
    And though the price as high again had been,
    We'd have paid it, bravely, for the Nation's sake.
    Comrades, sleep on, till God's great Spirit comes
    To clothe you with the life which never ends;
    And o'er this shell-swept, bruised, and bleeding land
    Victorious and enduring peace descends.

THE SILVER LINING

War in itself is not a blessing—neither is the surgeon's knife. If it were a choice between a slow, painful death from a malignant cancer, or an operation, which would give pain for the time being, but which ultimately would bring relief and complete recovery—invariably the choice would be in favour of the operation.

War is hell, but its prosecution as an effective means in arresting the development of the cancer of mad militarism was as essential as the use of the surgeon's knife to remove a malignant growth.

War is an ugly business—it is carnage and horror. The thought of man butchered by his brother, the thought of both sea and land stained with human blood, spilled by human hands, is too horrible for contemplation. Yet peace at the price we were asked to pay would have been, in its effects, considerably worse than war.

There are accruing to us individually, and to the Empire, blessings which possibly no other event (certainly not undisturbed tranquillity) than this unprecedented conflict could have created. There are compensations that are apt to be overlooked. To realize appreciably the compensatory effects in connexion with this conflict, it is necessary that we turn from the purely sordid and sad aspect to its spiritual and constructive side. The question, Has this war produced anything that would approximately counterbalance the arrest of industry and progress, waste of life at its prime, the desolation of hearts and homes, the devastation of property, and the incalculable measures of sorrow and suffering?—is permissible, and we forget not the atrocities on both land and sea, the deliberate violation of individual and international laws, and the fact that there is hardly a street without a loss, and scarce a heart without anxiety.

Throw this immeasurable pile of war-waste and colossal suffering into the scales of thoughtful contemplation, then heap into it as a counter-weight the blessings that have accrued, and the effect upon our minds must necessarily be to lead us to become more hopeful and less ungrateful.

The Empire has awakened out of her sleep—she is purging away the dross that has accumulated round her life, and at last as a nation we have found our soul.

The war found us in a muddle, both from a military and moral viewpoint, but out of that muddle a miracle has been fashioned. In addition, the Empire, even to its remotest outposts, has been consolidated, and the people over whom King George reigns are bound together in indissoluble bonds sealed with blood. Russia is now freed from the shackles of tyrannical oppression and autocratic domination; and the right to existence of the smaller nations has been powerfully endorsed.

There are other factors than those stated above which contribute no inconsiderable weight towards counter-balancing the load of hardship and heartaches that this war has heaped upon us. Such will be the theme of many writers when the smoke has lifted and the peoples of this earth again repose in the embrace of world-peace.

We have, so far, only briefly considered the beneficial effects of this war upon the Empire. When we come to consider what the war has done for the individual, particularly those who are actively engaged at the battle fronts, the difference between the weight of suffering and the weight of blessing will be very palpable, even to the most superficial mind.

Perhaps the blessing of most permanent importance that this war has brought to the majority of us is a strengthened faith in immortality. We cannot penetrate the veil that screens the mysteries of the future from our vision. Faith and the inner consciousness are the basis of our belief that there is a future. One cannot be at the Front very long before he is compelled to examine his thoughts in regard to immortality. Death is brought home very closely. The grim spectre points his finger at a man—perhaps in the first flush of manhood—who has just commenced to appreciate the joy of living. Death challenges, and with no shadow of faltering, but perhaps with a smile, the challenge is accepted, and the lad goes under. It is no triumph for death. It is the soul of a man that has gained a glorious victory. One feels convinced that it is but the body that has terminated existence. The physical presence is no more, but the personality—the soul—has been translated and passed beyond us. Freed from the limitations of this earthly life, it has passed into the infinite to be with others who have gone before.

Many scenes have been witnessed the memory of which, even now, fills the eyes with tears. Men waiting the advance of death—resolutely, fearless, hopeful.

The war has done in a few months what years of preaching apparently failed to effect. It has produced a revival of religion amongst men, and consequently a slump in ritualism. Christianity has always had its enemies, and any opportunity for adversely criticizing the system has been laid hold of by some with amazing alacrity. The report that the nearer men get to the firing line the less mindful they become of the claims of Christ is entirely false, and could only have been circulated by people who desired to depreciate the men whose character and courage command the admiration of all who know and understand them. Those responsible for the rise and spread of such a libel are neither the friends of the Church nor of the soldiers.

All soldiers are not saints; all may not be gentlemen. Such claim has never been made by them, nor has it ever been their well-wishers' boast. Yet there are many soldiers whose lives are clean and sweet, who are entitled to be described 'saints' if ever man was. As for what constitutes a 'gentleman,' a difference of opinion exists; but judged by the standard raised since the outset of this terrific conflict amongst the nations, I have no hesitation in affirming that the vast majority of them are 'Nature's own.'

Certainly there are some who are careless and callous, who are not and never were amenable to the claims of Christ, who daily grow more forgetful of home-ties and become slaves to ignoble appetites; but such are few, very few, indeed; and the like are to be seen not only in military but also in civil life, and generally are not unfamiliar with orderly or court-room proceedings. Is it right that all should be condemned because of the capricious behaviour of an infinitesimal section? Is it Christ-like to condemn those whose actions are called into question? Even they are not beyond the pale of reformation and redemption—for such Christ tasted death.

Then there are a few whose knowledge of the world and its wickedness is limited, who are separated from the restraints of home life, and who stray as sheep and sin in ignorance. Are all so strong that they can dispense with guidance, or so pure that sin ceases to allure? 'Let him who is without sin throw the first stone.'

The men in the main are better since they joined up, and evidence is not lacking that from the date of enlistment they appreciably realized the seriousness of the work to which they so willingly devoted themselves.

As they get nearer to, and while they are at, the Front, they become more reverent and less disposed to frivolity. All church parades are voluntary, and the chaplains have no occasion to complain about poor attendances. The men crowd the buildings used for gospel meetings, and large numbers of them have publicly acknowledged their acceptance of the Christian faith.

In proportion to the number of services conducted and the opportunities for attending them, more soldiers are present at religious meetings at the Front than civilians at home. In the ranks and amongst both N.C.O.'s and officers there are splendid Christian men. These men are a tower of strength to the chaplains, and their influence for good amongst their comrades is incalculable.

It has been whispered that the war has completely shattered the foundations of Christianity; but from close observation I am inclined to the opinion that it has exposed the instability and inadequacy of human creeds, and will eventually accomplish what the Churches have so lamentably failed to do.

The war is an indictment against divided Christendom. If Christians the world over had been united in 'the faith' and 'of one mind in the Lord,' this war would have been both impracticable and impossible.

Men on active service have grown indifferent not to Christ and His Church, but to human creeds and *our* brand of Christianity. Both have been proved impotent during the progress of this war.

We have heard much about Christian union; no evidence of such is noticeable at the Front—at least amongst the accredited representatives of the various religious organizations. Emphasis is placed upon denominationalism, and more heart-burnings have been caused amongst the men in consequence of the divisions amongst the Churches than amongst the home folks at the fancied increasing irreverence and indifference of the men regarding the things that are esteemed sacred. The men give evidence of being disposed to stand outside of all *human* creeds. Their query is not 'Are you a member of a certain religious organization?' but 'Are you a member of *TheChurch*?' Their views of Christianity are as simple as they are scriptural. The soldiers are beginning to realize that what matters most is not whether a man is a member of a certain Church, but *is hea Christian?* Just as the people of Russia have freed themselves of the yoke of autocratic government, so I predict that the most potent contribution towards bringing about Christian union will come not from the recognized leaders of the Churches, but from the soldiers on active service who have been impressed with the impotence of the existing system to bring about that condition which represents the ideal of Christianity, and the answer to our Lord's prayer, 'that all may be one in Him.'

If the Allies were to strive for peace and the overthrow of evil in the same manner as the Churches are seeking the overthrow of evil and the effecting of Christian union, they might well give up the conflict. Prolongation of the war and ultimate defeat could be the only issue.

Many have learned to know themselves better. They have been made cognizant of their weaknesses and their strength—what they are capable of and where they fall short.

Life at the Front affords unique opportunities for studying men. One is brought into such close contact with them. Every one is different, each having his own characteristics, his own eccentricities—each a distinct and separate personality. A man sees why this one succeeds and why that one fails—he succeeds himself, and learns to have confidence.

Perhaps he fails and learns humility, and, maybe, because he has failed at one job he is given another, and he finds that he can 'make good.' Few, if any, ever dreamed that they were capable of performing the tasks which are daily assumed by or assigned to them.

Following upon a man getting to know himself, he acquires a knowledge of others. This tends to bridge the gulf that society has created between men. Class distinction is virtually eliminated after a few months of camp and active service life. Classification is made on the basis of character rather than on that of social status. This turn of events cannot help but materially contribute to the solution of those problems which arise out of the vexed question of social inequalities.

Another effect which this war has produced, and which will prove an inestimable blessing, is that the home associations and the little joys of home life have become for all time our priceless possessions such as they never could otherwise.

Our loved ones are enshrined in our hearts as never before. We feel that their personalities are with us, helping us every day. We have become capable of greater love for them. We live for them. We fight for them. Yea, we would willingly die for them! And for many of us our thoughts, our deeds, our daily living is the result of a constant endeavour to be as they would have us.

So I feel that the world will be better because of this war. Dark as is the cloud that hovers over all, it has its silver lining, and the majority of soldiers subscribe to the sentiments of the Apostle Paul, who declared that the sufferings of this present time are not worthy to be compared with the glory which shall be revealed in us. 'For our light affliction, which is but for a moment, worketh for us a far more exceeding and eternal weight of glory.'

I feel that Australia will be a better land because of the experiences that so many of her sons have gone through. They have learned what their loved ones and what their homes mean to them. They have learned to appreciate the things most worth while, and will return with hearts full of love and thankfulness, more ready than ever before to devote their lives to the happiness of those who with bursting hearts watched them go; and ever prayed for their return.

'They also serve who only stand and wait.'

How true that is, and how we have realized it since we have been out here! We know that the wives, the mothers, the sweethearts, have had a harder time than any of us. We realize the long anxious time of waiting they have gone through, and know the magnificent part they have played in this world-wide war.

However dark things may appear now, the future is radiant with hope, and Australia's sons will return to their beloved land bigger and better men than when they left; and our country will be a nobler one because so many of her sons heard the call of the Motherland, and responded gloriously.

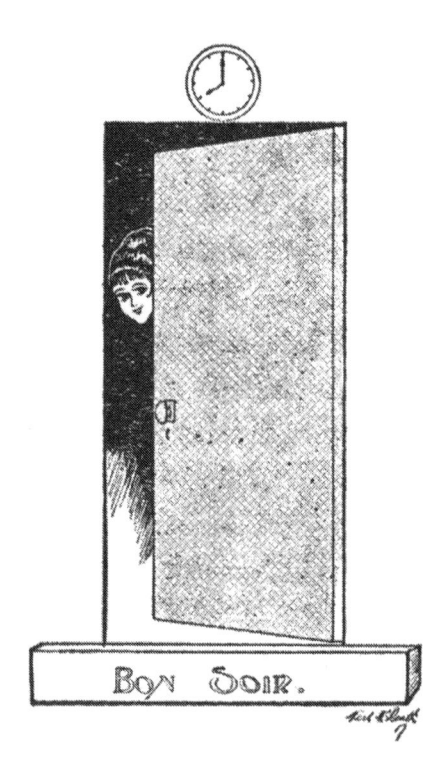

Printed by Jarrold & Sons, Ltd., Norwich, England.